ALASKA

Past and Present

Joanne Mattern

rosen publishing's
rosen
central®

New York

Published in 2011 by The Rosen Publishing Group, Inc.
29 East 21st Street, New York, NY 10010

Library of Congress Cataloging-in-Publication Data

Mattern, Joanne, 1963–
Alaska : past and present / Joanne Mattern. — 1st ed.
    p. cm. — (The United States : past and present)
Includes bibliographical references and index.
ISBN 978-1-4358-9475-4 (library binding) —
ISBN 978-1-4358-9503-4 (pbk.) —
ISBN 978-1-4358-9537-9 (6-pack)
1. Alaska—Juvenile literature. 2. Alaska—History—Juvenile literature. I. Title.
F904.3.M38 2011
979.8—dc22

                                                                    2009046615

Manufactured in Malaysia

CPSIA Compliance Information: Batch #S10YA: For further information, contact Rosen Publishing, New York, New York, at 1-800-237-9932.

On the cover: Top left: An Inuit prepares his sealskin kayak for going to sea. Top right: The Trans-Alaska Pipeline carries oil across 800 miles (1,287 kilometers) of Alaska's wilderness. Bottom: Tourists board a seaplane for a fishing trip near Anchorage.

Contents

Alaska is the largest U.S. state. It is located far from the mainland United States, off of northwestern Canada.

Introduction

Just about everything in Alaska is big and bold. It is the largest U.S. state by far, covering more land than the next three largest states combined. Alaska is home to the highest mountain in North America, as well as to glaciers, volcanoes, and other dramatic forces of nature. The state has a large population of animals, some of which are not found anywhere else in the United States. Imagine sharing your state with polar bears! Alaska's residents do just that.

Alaska is not physically connected to the rest of the United States, and it shares its only land border with Canada. Because of its remoteness and rugged landscape, Alaska has a very small population, especially when you consider its immense size.

Alaska's location gave it a different history than much of the rest of the country. However, there are many similarities as well. Like most other U.S. states, Alaska was first settled by Native Americans. Later, it attracted people who were searching for adventure and better lives for themselves and their families.

Alaska's uniqueness may be why this state has always captivated so many people. Thousands rushed to Alaska when gold was discovered in the late 1800s, and thousands more came when oil was discovered in the 1960s. Alaska's diverse residents have made the state a special part of America. Let's travel to the Last Frontier and learn what makes Alaska such an amazing place to live and work.

Chapter 1

THE LAND OF ALASKA

It's hard to imagine just how big Alaska is. It measures 586,412 square miles (1,518,800 square km) in land area, making it by far the largest U.S. state. It covers as much land as one-fifth of the forty-eight states on the mainland. Alaska is as large as Texas, California, and Montana put together.

Alaska also has unique borders. The country of Canada forms the state's eastern border. On the other three sides, Alaska is bordered by water, which makes it a peninsula. Alaska borders the Beaufort Sea and Arctic Ocean to the north and the Chukchi Sea to the northwest. The western part of Alaska borders the Bering Sea and the Bering Strait. The Gulf of Alaska and Pacific Ocean form the state's southern border. Russia is on the other side of the Bering Strait, only about 50 miles (80 km) west of Alaska. So Alaska is closer to two foreign countries than it is to the rest of the United States!

Alaska's Natural Regions

Alaska's land includes many different physical and natural features. The state is divided into five main regions: the Far North, the Interior, the Southwest, the Southcentral, and the Southeast.

Because the sun doesn't set during the long summer nights in the Far North, it is possible to see a rainbow at midnight!

Far North

The Far North of Alaska is also called the North Slope or the Arctic Coastal Plain. It stretches from the Arctic Ocean and Beaufort Sea in the north to the foothills of the mountains called the Brooks Range. Most of this region is located inside the Arctic Circle. Most of the land is tundra, and there is a layer of permafrost (permanently frozen soil) a few feet underground. No trees grow on the tundra, but grasses and flowers do bloom for a number of weeks every summer.

There are large deposits of oil and natural gas in the Far North. In addition, large areas have been set aside as national parkland, including the Gates of the Arctic National Park and Preserve and the Arctic National Wildlife Refuge.

Because of the region's extreme northern location, the sun does not set here during part of the summer. This feature gives Alaska one of its nicknames: Land of the Midnight Sun.

A climber stands alone at the top of Summit Ridge at Denali, North America's highest mountain.

Interior

The Interior is the central portion of the state and is home to Fairbanks, Alaska's second largest city. This area lies between two major mountain ranges, the Brooks Range and the Alaska Range. Denali, which used to be called Mount McKinley, is located in the Alaska Range. Denali is the highest mountain in North America, at 20,320 feet (6,194 meters). Between these two mountain ranges are several smaller mountain ranges and low, rolling hills. The Yukon River stretches across the region and into Canada.

Southwest

The Southwest region includes the Seward Peninsula, which stretches west to the Bering Strait. The city of Nome is located on this peninsula. Farther south, the land includes the Yukon and Kuskokwim river deltas.

Although this region has several mountain ranges, most of the land is wet and flat. There are numerous lakes and offshore islands.

Prince William Sound: Site of the Exxon Valdez Disaster

For thousands of years, Prince William Sound was a beautiful and pure natural landscape. The waters of the sound and the rocky beaches that surrounded it were home to a huge variety of wildlife, including whales, seabirds, otters, and fish. The area's beauty changed in an instant on March 24, 1989, when the oil tanker *Exxon Valdez* ran aground. The accident tore open the bottom of the ship and poured almost eleven million gallons (almost forty-one million liters) of oil into the water. The result was one of the most devastating environmental disasters in history.

The oil spill polluted the sound with millions of gallons of thick oil. The oil spread for miles before people could even try to contain and remove it, and the pollution worsened during the days that followed. Not only was the water polluted, but oil also washed up on the shores, coating rocks and soaking into the sand. In the end, more than 11,000 square miles (28,480 sq km) of ocean were affected.

The spill had a disastrous effect on wildlife. Scientists estimate that more than 250,000 seabirds were killed, along with 2,800 sea otters, plus river otters and orcas. The oil destroyed billions of salmon and herring eggs, and it spoiled fish-hatching grounds for years.

Today, more than twenty years after the disaster, Prince William Sound looks a lot like it did before the oil spill. The water looks clean and so do the beaches, and animals have returned to the area. However, experts estimate that it will take at least another ten years for all of the contamination to disappear. A 2007 study found that more than 27,000 gallons (more than 102,000 liters) of oil are still present in the soil along the shoreline. Local animals are still showing health effects from the spill, and there are a reduced number of fish and eggs in the area. The *Exxon Valdez* disaster is a powerful example of how human carelessness can destroy natural beauty, perhaps forever.

Kodiak Island in the Gulf of Alaska is the second largest island in the United States after the island of Hawaii.

The Southwest region also includes the Alaska Peninsula and the Aleutian Islands. These areas stretch in a long, curving line almost 1,400 miles (2,253 km) into the Pacific Ocean. Most of the islands were formed by volcanic eruptions long ago, and the islands are small, round, and rocky. The area is still a hotbed of volcanic activity today.

Southcentral

Located just above the Gulf of Alaska, the Southcentral region includes the Cook Inlet, Prince William Sound, and the Kenai Peninsula in between. The city of Anchorage is located at the northeast end of the Cook Inlet. More than half of Alaska's population lives in the region. The climate is milder in this area because of its southern location and because it is near warm ocean currents. However, extreme conditions can still occur here.

There are many glaciers in the region, as well as at least ten active volcanoes. In the eastern part of the region, Wrangell-St. Elias National Park and Preserve contains numerous mountain peaks of more than 16,000 feet (4,877 m).

Icy waters surround islands near Glacier Bay National Park in Southeast Alaska.

Southeast

Southeast Alaska is also known as the Panhandle. The

Panhandle is a narrow strip of land that stretches south and east toward British Columbia, Canada. The region is bordered on the west by the Pacific Ocean. Juneau, the state capital, is located in this region and can only be reached by boat or by air.

The area has a wet and mild climate, rocky shorelines, tall mountains, and forests. There are more than one thousand islands off the coast. A large inlet of water called the Inside Passage is a major transportation and tourist corridor. The Inside Passage contains many fjords, or channels between tall cliffs. Glacier Bay National Park is located in the northern part of the region.

Animal Life

Alaska has a huge variety of animal life. The state is home to large mammals such as bears, wolves, mountain goats, caribou, moose, musk oxen, and more. Smaller mammals include arctic foxes and hares. There are also a great variety of birds in Alaska. These birds include snowy owls, bald eagles, puffins, ravens, falcons, ducks, swans, and many types of geese. Millions of migrating birds travel through Alaska and nest there in the summer.

A mother grizzly bear leads her cubs through a lake in Katmai National Park and Preserve.

The waters off Alaska are full of animal life. Fifteen species of whales live in the waters bordering the state, including humpback whales, blue whales, gray whales, and orcas. Walruses, sea lions, and seals also live in Alaska's waters, as do five species of salmon. More salmon live in Alaska than in any other part of the world.

Plant Life

Although Alaska has a harsh climate, many types of plants manage to thrive in the state. The tundra is covered with mosses and lichens during the short summer. About one-quarter of the state is forested. The interior forests are called taiga. These evergreen forests begin where the tundra ends and include birch and spruce trees. Southern Alaska also has boreal forests—northern forests that include larger birches, spruces, and cottonwoods. Other trees in Alaska include willows, alders, cedars, and hemlocks.

Summer brings an explosion of colorful flowers to the state, including lupines, larkspur, wild asters, fireweed, and violets. Alaska also produces wild berries, including lingonberries, blueberries, cranberries, and strawberries. More than five hundred kinds of wild mushrooms grow in the state.

Chapter 2

THE HISTORY OF ALASKA

Thousands of years ago, Alaska was connected to Siberia by a land bridge. More than twelve thousand years ago, the first settlers walked across that bridge and became Alaska's first residents.

Alaska's Native People

Alaska's first residents, called Paleo-Indians by scholars, were hunter-gatherers. The men hunted seals, whales, caribou, and other large animals, while the women gathered berries, nuts, and roots.

Later, Alaska's native people belonged to a number of different groups. These groups came to Alaska in different waves of migration and spread out to different parts of the land. The Aleuts lived in villages on the Aleutian Islands. The men fished and hunted using boats that were similar to kayaks. The Inuit (also known as the Inupiat, Inupiaq, Yupik, and Eskimo) lived along Alaska's coastlines. In winter, the Inuit lived in sod houses lined with whale bones, stones, or driftwood. They also built igloos for shelter. In the summers, they lived in tents made of seal or caribou skins.

The Athabascan Indians lived in Alaska's interior. They did not build permanent settlements. Instead, they followed herds of caribou and moose, or they fished for salmon. Other Native American

Walruses were an important source of food for Alaska's native people. A group of Inuit drag a walrus to their village in this picture, taken around 1930.

tribes, including the Tlingit, Haida, and Tsimshian, lived in south-eastern Alaska. As part of their religion and culture, these tribes created elaborate artwork on totem poles, ceremonial costumes, blankets, and everyday objects.

The Russians Are Coming

For centuries, the native peoples had Alaska to themselves. However, the Russians were interested in exploring this nearby land. In 1728, Peter the Great, the tsar (ruler) of Russia, sent Vitus Bering to explore Alaska. Bering was a Danish officer serving in the Russian navy. He became the first European to sail across the narrow strait separating Russia and North America. However, bad weather and ice prevented him from going ashore.

Bering returned to the area in 1741. This time, he was able to explore several islands off Alaska's southern coast. Bering died during this journey, but his men brought sea otter skins and sealskins back to Russia. These skins and furs were very valuable, and they increased Russia's interest in going to Alaska. Soon many traders and adventurers were crossing the Bering Strait to this new land.

The arrival of the Russians was devastating to Alaska's native population. The Aleuts were especially hard-hit. They had no immunity to the diseases carried by the Russians, so many died of illness. Also, the Russian traders forced the Aleut men to trap furs for them, and they abused and killed many of the native people. The Aleuts tried to resist, attacking the Russians a number of times in the early 1760s. However, the Russian traders had firearms and simply brought in more force. In 1784, Russia established its first permanent settlement on Kodiak Island.

In 1799, Russia's tsar put a fur-trading firm called the Russian American Company in charge of Alaska. The tsar appointed Aleksandr Baranov, a Russian merchant, as the company's manager and governor of the colony. Baranov made the city of Sitka the company's headquarters. The Tlingit briefly drove the Russians out of Sitka with a battle in 1802. However, by 1804, Baranov and his men had overcome native resistance and won control of the southeastern part of Alaska.

Seward's Folly

Russia was not the only country interested in Alaska's riches. Explorers also came from other nations, including Great Britain,

Secretary of State William Seward's purchase of Alaska for $7.2 million was a great deal for the United States. This check from the U.S. Treasury was used to purchase the territory.

Spain, and France. British explorer Captain James Cook reached the area in 1778. He created maps that were so detailed that explorers used them for the next one hundred years.

Russia was not happy about the increasing presence of the British and others in Alaska. However, Russia had too many other problems to focus on defending the area. Russia also saw that keeping a colony was expensive and that fur profits had declined. As a result, Russia decided to sell the colony to the United States in 1867. Secretary of State William H. Seward realized the United States could benefit from acquiring Alaska's vast timber, mineral, and animal resources. Seward arranged for the United States to buy Alaska for $7.2 million. That worked out to only two cents an acre!

Many people thought the purchase was ridiculous and that Seward had made a big mistake. They thought Alaska was nothing more than a vast wasteland covered with ice and snow. These people came up with a new nickname for the territory. They called it Seward's folly. However, Seward believed he had gotten a great deal, and it turned out he was right.

Gold!

A few of Alaska's settlers had found gold deposits over the years. In 1880, two prospectors named Joe Juneau and Richard Harris, along with a Tlingit chief as a guide, found a large deposit of gold in Southeast Alaska. Word of the discovery spread throughout the United States. Suddenly, everyone wanted to go to Alaska! Prospectors and adventurers rushed to Alaska, hoping to find a fortune.

Settlers begin the difficult journey to the Klondike gold fields during the Gold Rush of 1897–1898. The Chilkoot Trail out of Dyea, Alaska, was a popular stampede route.

Although very few people got rich from mining gold, some settlers got rich by selling goods to the prospectors. Towns sprang up around the gold camps, and businesses were set up to sell food, clothing, tools, and supplies. The city of Juneau, named after Joe Juneau, was founded during that area's gold rush. Nome was founded when gold was discovered there in 1898. Between 1897 and 1900, thousands rushed to Alaska in order to reach gold fields in Canada's Yukon Territory. The Alaskan towns of Skagway and Dyea became boomtowns as the "stampeders" flooded in on steamships. This period became known as the Klondike Gold Rush.

Between 1880 and 1900, Alaska's population almost doubled, from thirty-two thousand people to sixty-three thousand people. The

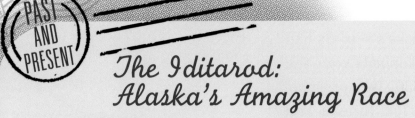

The Iditarod: Alaska's Amazing Race

The Inuit first developed dog mushing (using a team of dogs to pull a sled) as a way to travel across heavy snow. For hundreds of years, dog mushing was an important part of everyday life. The Inuit made sleds out of whale and caribou bones. The runners were layers of mud and moss, made smooth with a coating of freezing water.

Later, Russian and then American settlers followed their example, using teams of dogs to pull sleds loaded with supplies. One of the most famous trails was the Iditarod Trail. In the early twentieth century, the trail was a valuable link to remote parts of Alaska in the winter when river travel was impossible. A musher with a large dog team could move more than 1,000 pounds (454 kilograms) of freight and mail.

Dog mushing proved to be lifesaving in 1925, when residents of Nome faced an outbreak of a deadly disease called diphtheria. The town needed medicine, and the most reliable way to get it there was by dogsled. First, a train carried the medicine from Anchorage to the town of Nenana. From there, twenty of Alaska's best mushers ran a relay of more than 700 miles (1,126 km) through blizzards and other dangerous conditions. The medicine arrived in Nome six days later, in time to save the town. The event became famous all over the world.

Today, people can travel throughout Alaska by snowmobile and airplane. However, dog mushing is still a popular sport, and dozens of races are held in Alaska every year. The most famous is the Iditarod Trail Sled Dog Race. It began in 1973 to commemorate the historic race to Nome, as well as the overall role that sled dogs played in Alaska's history. During the Iditarod, teams of sled dogs and their mushers travel more than 1,000 miles (1,609 km) from Anchorage to Nome, a journey that takes more than a week. Competitors use modern sleds made of ash, plastic, and fiberglass, and they work with dogs that are bred and trained for racing. The routine of racing is very different from the use of dogsleds just to get around. However, the spirit of dog mushing has remained the same.

rising number of settlers led to the development of schools, churches, and hospitals. Regular mail delivery began. Steamboat and dogsled routes allowed supplies to reach remote areas.

In 1912, Alaska officially became a U.S. territory. In 1914, the government built a railroad to connect mining areas with growing cities such as Juneau, which had become the territory's capital.

World War II

When World War II began, Alaska was vulnerable to attack because of its location near Asia. In June 1942, Japanese bombs hit Dutch Harbor in the Aleutian Islands. Even more alarming, Japanese forces invaded two of the islands, Attu and Kiska. Japan's army occupied the islands for more than a year before the U.S. military forced them out in August 1943. After the invasion, the United States evacuated the Aleutian Islands and forced its residents to live in camps in Southeast Alaska until the war ended. Although this action was taken to protect the residents, conditions were so harsh in the camps that many Aleuts died.

At the time of the invasion, Alaska could only be reached by ship or airplane. The federal government wanted to link the U.S. mainland to Alaska to make it easier to send troops and supplies. Starting in 1942, the U.S. Army Corps of Engineers built the Alaska Highway (also known as the Alaska-Canadian, or Alcan, Highway) in an amazing eight months. The highway links Dawson Creek in British Columbia to Delta Junction, Alaska, and stretches for about 1,500 miles (2,414 km). The highway is still the only road to link Alaska to the "lower forty-eight" states.

The government improved other forms of infrastructure, too, and moved a large number of military and civilian workers to Alaska. This flow of people continued even after the war ended.

The construction of the Alaska Highway was one of Alaska's greatest transportation projects. This photo shows a tractor widening the road after it was cut through the forest.

State Number Forty-Nine

By 1950, more than 128,000 people lived in Alaska. Many residents felt it was time the territory became a U.S. state. In 1955, Alaskans chose delegates to draft a state constitution. Once the constitution was approved, Alaska applied to the federal government for statehood. The U.S. Congress passed the Alaska Statehood Act in 1958. Then it was up to the voters. On August 26, 1958, Alaska's residents voted to approve statehood by an overwhelming margin of five to one. On January 3, 1959, Alaska officially became the forty-ninth state.

During its first decade of statehood, two major events changed Alaska forever. On March 27, 1964, a powerful earthquake struck Prince William Sound and the surrounding area, including the city of Anchorage. The earthquake measured 9.2 on the Richter scale, making it one of the most powerful quakes ever recorded. More than one hundred people were killed, and property damage totaled more than $300 million.

In 1968, a huge oil deposit was discovered in Prudhoe Bay on the North Slope. The state built a pipeline to connect the remote oilfields to the port of Valdez, and it sold rights to the oil to several corporations. The discovery of oil and the building of the pipeline brought millions of dollars to Alaska, but, it also changed the natural landscape.

Alaska in the Twenty-First Century

Alaska remains in a strong position today, but the state also faces many challenges. Its economy is closely tied to the oil industry. Changes in the demand for oil affect the amount of money that the state receives, as well as employment opportunities. Today, Americans continue to debate how much of Alaska's land and water should be preserved as wilderness and how much should be opened up for oil drilling.

Also, Alaskan's continue to debate the rights of Alaska's native peoples. State government and tribal leaders are trying to work together to create better living conditions for all of Alaska's residents.

Chapter 3

THE GOVERNMENT OF ALASKA

Juneau became Alaska's territorial capital in 1900. It became the state capital in 1959, when Alaska became the forty-ninth state. It is the only state capital that shares a border with another country—Canada.

Alaska's state capital may be unique, but its government is set up very much like the federal government and like other states' systems. Alaska's government has three branches: the executive branch, the legislative branch, and the judicial branch. These three branches follow rules set out in the state's constitution.

The Executive Branch

The executive branch carries out state laws. Alaska's executive branch includes the governor and the lieutenant governor. Both of these officials are elected to four-year terms.

Alaska's governor is very powerful. He or she appoints all of the state's top officials. These officials include the attorney general, district attorneys, and judges. The governor also appoints the heads of fourteen major state departments, including corrections, health and social services, labor, and environmental conservation. These departments are part of the executive branch, too.

If the governor cannot serve, the lieutenant governor takes his or her place. The lieutenant governor is responsible for supervising state elections and running the Alaska Historical Commission, along with other duties that support and help the governor.

This house has served as the Alaska Governor's Mansion since 1912. It is the official residence of the governor and his or her family.

The Legislative Branch

The job of the legislative branch is to make and pass laws. The legislature also approves the state budget. Like many other states, Alaska has a legislature with two houses. The upper house is called the senate. The lower house is called the house of representatives.

Alaska's senate has twenty members. These members are elected every four years. Alaska's house of representatives has forty members, who are elected to two-year terms. Any member of the legislature can propose a new law, or bill. If a majority of the legislators vote to approve the bill, it goes to the governor to be signed into law. The governor can veto, or reject, any bill, but the legislature has the opportunity to override the veto and put the law into effect.

Alaska's legislature has one unusual responsibility. Alaska is not divided into counties with local governments. Instead, one-third of the state is divided into sixteen units called boroughs. Each borough has its own local government. The other two-thirds of the state have no local government because the population is so small and is spread out over such a huge area. Instead, the state legislature governs this area.

PAST
AND
PRESENT

The Rights of Native People

For many years, Alaska's native people had little or no say in Alaska's government. They did not even have control over many aspects of their daily lives. In the 1800's, many missionaries and educators thought the best way to treat Alaska's native people was to teach them to be part of the white culture. In some schools, natives were forbidden to speak their own languages or celebrate their cultural traditions. During the early 1900s, Alaska had legal segregation. Much like African Americans in the South, Alaska Natives were not allowed to enter certain stores, restaurants, hotels, and other businesses.

Obvious discrimination such as this ended in 1945, when the state passed the Anti-Discrimination Act. However, natives were still treated unfairly, especially in terms of controlling the land. Alaska Natives were angry that the government took away much of their land in order to create national parks and wildlife preserves. In addition, when oil was discovered on the North Slope, land was given to oil corporations without any concern about the rights of the native people who had lived in the area for centuries.

Alaska Natives protested to the federal government for many years. Finally, in 1971, the U.S. Congress passed the Alaska Native Claims Settlement Act, or ANCSA. This law gave forty-four million acres (eighteen million hectares) of land back to Alaska's native people. In addition, Alaska Natives received more than $962 million as payment for land that had been taken away from them. ANCSA also allowed natives to form their own corporations to control their land and their income. This law led to the creation of many native-run companies that operate mines, lumber mills, fisheries, and other industries.

In recent years, Alaska's government has reached out to the natives with the passage of new agreements. The Millennium Agreement of 2001 set up procedures for the state to work with tribal governments in order to create better education opportunities and more public services for them and to give native communities more of a voice in state affairs.

The Judicial Branch

The judicial branch is the state's court system. Alaska's court system has four levels. District courts handle minor cases at the local level. These courts also issue marriage licenses and other legal documents. The next level is the superior court. The superior court handles more serious criminal and civil cases, as well as any case that involves children. The third level is the court of appeals. This court has three judges who hear appeals from district or superior courts. An appeals court can reverse any decision made by a lower court.

Dozens of lawyers listen in the courtroom during a trial in Alaska Superior Court. The superior court handles serious civil and criminal cases.

Alaska's highest court is the supreme court. The state's supreme court includes one chief justice and four justices. These judges make sure that Alaska's laws follow the state constitution. Decisions made by the lower courts can be appealed at the supreme court level.

Chapter 4

THE ECONOMY OF ALASKA

Alaska's economy has changed dramatically over the past one hundred years. But one thing has stayed the same: Alaska depends on natural resources for a large part of its industry.

Oil and Mining

Oil explorers discovered oil fields on the Kenai Peninsula in 1957. A much larger deposit was found on the North Slope in 1968. In the 1970s, oil companies built the Trans-Alaska Pipeline System to carry oil from the North Slope to the port of Valdez in southern Alaska. From there, tankers could ship the oil to the mainland.

The construction of the pipeline created many jobs and opportunities. Alaska's oil industry employs thousands of workers in oil fields, along the pipeline, in refineries, and in shipping. Today, oil is the most important source of the state's income. About eighty-five cents of every dollar that the state earns comes from oil.

In the late 1800s, thousands of people rushed to Alaska to mine gold. Today, gold mining is a very small part of the state's economy, but Alaska does still mine it and several other mineral resources. Silver, coal, tin, copper, and lead are all mined in the state. Alaska is also the world's largest producer of zinc.

Fishing and Farming

Of the fifty states, Alaska produces the most seafood. Alaska's fisheries produce more than 5 billion pounds (2.3 billion kg) of fish and shellfish each year. Salmon is Alaska's most important fish, but the state produces pollack, herring, halibut, shrimp, and crab, too. Commercial fishing also supports other businesses, such as factories and canneries that process, pack, and ship the seafood.

Agriculture is not a large part of Alaska's economy, but the state supports about five hundred farms. Major crops include hay, potatoes, barley, oats, and vegetables. Most farms are located in the central part of the state. The region's relatively long summer and mild weather produce vegetables of record size.

A fisherman helps bring in a net full of sockeye salmon on a boat near Bristol Bay. Salmon fishing is one of the most important industries in Alaska.

Service and Tourism

As with most other states, the service industry is a major part of Alaska's economy. This industry includes people who work in stores, banks, hospitals, offices, and schools.

Tourism has become a very important part of Alaska's service industry and overall economy. Millions of tourists come to see

Alaska's Oil Industry

In 1968, a new kind of gold was discovered in Alaska: oil. Like the gold rush of the previous century, the discovery of oil in Prudhoe Bay created a rush of people and corporations who were eager to benefit from the riches that were found there.

In order to transport the oil, the Trans-Alaska Pipeline was built after years of debate. Completed in 1977, the pipeline was 800 miles (1,287 km) long and cost $8 billion to build. The construction of the pipeline presented some unique challenges. To avoid damaging the permafrost, a pipeline carrying hot oil could not run underground. Instead, it had to be held aloft by metal supports and cables. Also, to complete the journey from Prudhoe Bay to Valdez, the pipeline had to cross three mountain ranges, as well as many rivers and streams. Many environmental groups were concerned that the pipeline would damage or destroy the wilderness habitat. Luckily, animals and plants have not been greatly affected by the giant pipe running through the landscape.

Today, oil dominates Alaska's economy, playing an important role in the state's financial health. There are a few reasons for this. First, Alaska sold oil-drilling rights to several oil companies. These companies pay Alaska to drill the oil and transport it out of the state. In addition, the oil and construction industries were able to add a large number of jobs in oil drilling, processing, and shipping. Today, the oil industry pumps so much money into Alaska's economy that residents do not have to pay a state income tax. Also, Alaska's residents receive yearly payments from the state's Permanent Fund. The state government created this fund to invest money earned from the North Slope oil fields. It is intended to provide a source of income if the oil fields ever run dry. Every year, the state pays part of the interest on the Permanent Fund to every resident who has lived in the state for at least one year.

The Trans-Alaska Pipeline follows the shape of the land on its journey across Alaska.

Alaska's natural wonders every year. These tourists support thousands of jobs in stores, restaurants, and hotels. The cruise ships that travel up and down the Inside Passage also hire thousands of workers. Tourists visit national parks, wilderness areas, museums, historical sites, zoos, and other attractions. All of these employ many people in Alaska.

Visitors enjoy a spectacular view of Skilak Lake in the Kenai National Wildlife Refuge. Millions of tourists come to enjoy Alaska's wilderness every year.

The Government and the Military

About 29 percent of Alaskans work for their federal, state, or local government, making the government one of the state's largest single employers. The U.S. government has a stronger presence in Alaska than in many states. The federal government is the largest landholder in the state and controls most of Alaska's wild areas.

The U.S. military is another major employer in Alaska. Soldiers guard the Trans-Alaska Pipeline, as well as missile sites in the state. Military personnel are also stationed in Alaska because it is so close to Russia and other nations in Asia. The U.S. Coast Guard has a major presence in Alaska and often performs search-and-rescue operations in the waters in and around the state.

Chapter 5

PEOPLE FROM ALASKA:
PAST AND PRESENT

Some of America's most fascinating people have called Alaska home. From athletes to artists, religious leaders to politicians, here are a few of Alaska's most famous residents.

E. L. "Bob" Bartlett (1904–1968) Born in Seattle, Washington, Bob Bartlett went to college in Fairbanks. He worked as a newspaper reporter there before entering politics. He served as Alaska's territorial delegate to the U.S. Congress from 1945 to 1959. After Alaska became a state in 1959, Bartlett served as a senator from Alaska until his death in 1968. He is often called the Architect of Alaska Statehood because he was a leading figure in the struggle to make Alaska a U.S. state.

Irene Bedard (1967–) Irene Bedard spent her early childhood in Anchorage. A Native American, Bedard has played native characters in movies and on television. She is perhaps best known as the voice of Pocahontas in the Disney animated movie of the same name. Bedard has also performed voices in cartoons such as *What's New, Scooby-Doo?*, *Pepper Ann*, and *The Real Adventures of Johnny Quest*.

Carlos Boozer (1981–) Carlos Boozer grew up in Juneau. He won many awards while playing basketball in high school and was named Alaska's Player of the Year three times. Boozer joined the National Basketball Association (NBA) in 2002, and he has played for the Cleveland Cavaliers and Utah Jazz.

Susan Butcher and her dog team arrive triumphantly in Nome, winning the 1990 Iditarod race.

Susan Butcher (1954–2006) Susan Butcher was born in Boston, but she moved to Alaska in 1975 to raise sled dogs. She became the first person to win three Iditarod races in a row, in 1986, 1987, and 1988. She won the race again in 1990. Butcher and her family lived in Eureka.

Carl Ben Eielson (1897–1929) Born in North Dakota, Carl Eielson became a pilot and moved to Alaska when he was twenty-two years old. In 1924, he made the first Alaska airmail flight, taking only four hours to fly from Fairbanks to McGrath. In 1928, he became a national hero as the first person to fly over the Arctic Ocean. Eielson was killed in a plane crash in 1929 while on a rescue mission to help an icebound Russian ship.

Scott Gomez (1979–) Scott Gomez was born and grew up in Anchorage, where he enjoyed playing hockey. He became

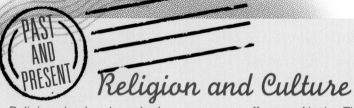

Religion and Culture

Religious leaders have had an enormous effect on Alaska. The first missionaries arrived from Russia in the 1800s. These Russian Orthodox missionaries opened many schools and churches. One of the most famous missionaries was Ivan Veniaminov. He volunteered to serve in the Aleutian Islands in 1821, when he was twenty-four years old. Veniaminov built a church and paddled a boat between the islands to visit the native people who lived there. He learned the native languages and taught residents about the Russian Orthodox faith. Veniaminov translated religious material into native languages, and he taught Alaskan natives how to read and write.

Protestant Christian missionaries also had a large influence on Alaska's population. Educators such as Sheldon Jackson and ministers such as Peter Trimble Rowe spread Christianity throughout Alaska and built churches, schools, and hospitals.

Today, there is still some evidence of the work of these early missionaries. For example, about 8 percent of the state's population belongs to the Russian Orthodox Church, a larger percentage than in any other state. However, technology has changed the way religious leaders communicate with their parishes today. One to two hundred years ago, missionaries could only travel by boat or dogsled. These men often faced brutal conditions as they traveled miles through remote areas in fierce winter storms and bitterly cold temperatures. Today, religious leaders can reach their parishioners over the Internet or by using television or radio. Traveling is also easier, thanks to snowmobiles and other vehicles.

However, organized religion does not seem to be as important to Alaskans now as in the past. A 2008 study found that Alaska is one of the least religious states. The population has low rates of church attendance and other behaviors related to organized religion. Some believe Alaska's independent spirit may extend to religion. In other words, Alaskans may want to find what works for them, rather than follow a set tradition or join a specific group. With so many different options and a lot more freedom than was available during the 1800s, Alaskans today can follow their hearts when it comes to spiritual matters.

the first Latino player in the National Hockey League (NHL) when he was drafted by the New Jersey Devils in 1999. Gomez was the NHL's Rookie of the Year in 2000, and he helped the Devils win two Stanley Cups in 2000 and 2003.

Sheldon Jackson (1834–1919) An educator and missionary, Sheldon Jackson came to Alaska in 1884 to open churches and schools throughout the territory. He served as the U.S. superintendent of public instruction in Alaska from 1885 to 1908. He is also famous for bringing reindeer to Alaska, where they were trained to pull sleds through heavy snow.

Jewel Kilcher (1974–) The popular folk and pop singer who simply calls herself Jewel emerged on the music scene after releasing her first album in 1995. Her hit songs include "Who Will Save Your Soul," "Foolish Games," and "You Were Meant for Me." Born in Utah, she moved to Alaska as a child and grew up in Homer and Anchorage. Jewel has also published books of poetry and acted in several movies.

Singer Jewel performs for excited fans at a concert in Florida. Jewel grew up in Alaska.

Trajan Langdon (1976–) Basketball player Trajan Langdon was born in California, but he moved to Anchorage when his father accepted a position at the University of Alaska. After a brief career as a minor league baseball player, Langdon switched sports and played for the NBA's Cleveland Cavaliers from 1999 to 2001. He was the first Alaskan to play in the NBA.

Austin Lathrop (1865–1950) Born in Wisconsin, Austin Lathrop moved to Alaska during the gold rush years. He started a business taking prospectors and their supplies to and from Alaska on his steamship. Lathrop became one of Alaska's most successful industrialists, with businesses in coal mining, lumber, transportation, banking, construction, and entertainment. He also started the first network of radio stations in Alaska and was active in politics.

Sydney Laurence (1865–1940) Sydney Laurence was born in Brooklyn, New York, where he studied art. He moved to Alaska in 1904 and worked as a prospector for several years before resuming his art career. Laurence became one of Alaska's most popular and well-known artists. He specialized in painting scenes of natural beauty, particularly Denali and the wilderness.

Hilary Lindh (1969–) Hilary Lindh was born in Juneau and began skiing when she was just two years old. She joined the U.S. Ski Team at age fourteen, and she went on to win a silver medal in downhill skiing at the 1992 Olympic Games.

Author Jack London described the harsh life of Alaska's gold rush settlers and their sled dogs. Readers still enjoy his exciting stories today.

Jack London (1876–1916) Jack London was born in San Francisco, California, but he traveled to Alaska in 1897 to take part in the gold rush. He became one of the most popular novelists of his time. London is best known for his tales of survival in the Alaskan wilderness. His most famous book, *The Call of the Wild*, describes the adventures of Buck, a dog who is kidnapped and becomes a sled dog in Alaska.

Sarah Palin (1964–) Sarah Palin was born in Idaho, but she came to Alaska when she was a baby. Palin started her

Sarah Palin speaks before a crowd of supporters during her vice-presidential race in 2008. Palin resigned as Alaska's governor in 2009 but continues to be a national figure.

political career as mayor of Wasilla. She became Alaska's first female, and youngest, governor when she was elected in 2006. She gained national attention in 2008, when she ran for vice president on John McCain's presidential ticket.

Libby Riddles (1956–) Libby Riddles was the first woman to win the Iditarod. She was born in Wisconsin, but she moved to Alaska when she was seventeen to raise and train sled dogs. Riddles entered her first Iditarod in 1980 and won the race in 1985. Riddles continues to live in Alaska, where she raises and trains dogs and writes books.

Leonhard Seppala (1877–1966) Leonhard Seppala became an Alaskan hero as one of the dogsled mushers who raced to Nome with medicine for a diphtheria outbreak. Born in Norway, Seppala came to Alaska as a young man to work as a gold prospector. He was already famous as a dog musher and breeder when he was asked to take part in the lifesaving run to Nome in 1925.

Deb Vanasse (1957–) Deb Vanasse was born in Minnesota, but she moved to Alaska to become a teacher. She has lived in Nunapitchuk, Bethel, and Fairbanks. Vanasse is best known as a children's author. Her books include *A Distant Enemy*, *Out of the Wilderness*, and *Under Alaska's Midnight Sun*.

Timeline

12,000–4000 BCE Ancestors of the Alaska Natives travel to Alaska from Asia over a land bridge.

1741 Vitus Bering, the first European in Alaska, lands on Kayak Island.

1778 British explorer Captain James Cook travels and maps the Alaskan coast.

1784 Russians build a settlement at Three Saints Bay on Kodiak Island.

1799 The Russian American Company is given control of Alaska.

1867 Russia sells Alaska to the United States for $7.2 million.

1880 Gold is found near present-day Juneau.

1900 Juneau becomes Alaska's capital.

1912 Alaska becomes a U.S. territory.

1914 The first railroad is built in Alaska.

1942 During World War II, Japanese forces occupy the islands of Attu and Kiska.

1943 The Alaska Highway is completed.

1955 Alaska drafts a state constitution.

1959 Alaska becomes the forty-ninth state.

1964 A powerful earthquake strikes Anchorage and the surrounding areas.

1968 Large oil deposits are discovered in Prudhoe Bay on the North Slope.

1971 The Alaska Native Claims Settlement Act is passed.

1977 The Trans-Alaska Pipeline is completed.

1980 The U.S. Congress adds 104 million acres (42 million ha) of Alaska's land to the National Park System.

1989 The *Exxon Valdez* runs aground and spills eleven million gallons (almost forty-one million liters) of oil in Prince William Sound.

2001 The Millennium Act is passed.

2006 Sarah Palin, the state's first female governor, takes office.

State motto:	"North to the Future"
State capital:	Juneau
State song:	"Alaska's Flag"
State flower:	Forget-me-not
State bird:	Willow ptarmigan
State tree:	Sitka spruce
State fish:	King salmon
State insect:	Four-spot skimmer dragonfly
State mineral:	Gold
State gem:	Jade
State fossil:	Woolly mammoth
State sport:	Dog mushing
Statehood date and number:	January 3, 1959; forty-ninth state
State nicknames:	The Last Frontier; Land of the Midnight Sun
Total area and U.S. rank:	663,267 square miles (1,717,854 sq km), including land and water; the largest state

State Flag

State Seal

Population: 626,932 (2000 census)

Length of coastline: 6,640 miles (10,624 km)

Length of shoreline: 33,904 miles (54,563 km), including islands

Highest elevation: Denali, 20,320 feet (6,194 m)

Lowest elevation: Sea level at the Pacific Ocean

Major rivers: Colville River, Kenai River, Kuskokwim River, Kobuk River, Noatak River, Tanana River, Yukon River

Major lakes: Becharof Lake, Iliamna Lake, Teshekpuk Lake, Naknek Lake

Hottest temperature recorded: 100 degrees Fahrenheit (38 degrees Celsius) at Fort Yukon, on June 27, 1915

Coldest temperature recorded: -80° F (-62° C) at Prospect Creek, on January 23, 1971

Origin of state name: From the Aleut word *alyeska*, meaning "great land"

Chief agricultural products: Greenhouse and nursery plants, aquaculture, dairy products, livestock, poultry, eggs, hay, barley

Chief mineral resources: Petroleum, natural gas, zinc, gold, lead, silver, copper, coal, sand, gravel, clay

Major industries: Commercial fishing, oil/petroleum, lumber, mining, furs, tourism

Willow ptarmigan

Forget-me-not

GLOSSARY

agriculture The practice of farming.

boreal Of or belonging to the forest areas of the north. Boreal forests contain cone-bearing trees, such as spruce, fir, and pine.

constitution Basic laws that establish and run a government. These laws guarantee certain rights to the people.

delta Flat area of land where a river empties into the sea.

evacuate To remove people from a dangerous area in an organized way.

executive Having to do with the branch of government that carries out laws and runs public affairs.

federal Having to do with the national government.

fjord A long, narrow inlet of the sea bordered by steep cliffs.

glacier A slow-moving mass of ice.

immunity Resistance to disease.

judicial Having to do with judges and courts.

legislative Having to do with making laws.

lichen An organism made up of a fungus and an algae that grow in union.

mainland The main landmass of a country or region.

missionary A person who is sent to convert others to a religion and to do humanitarian work.

native Having to do with people who originally live in an area.

parishioner Member of a local church.

peninsula A body of land surrounded by water on three sides.

permafrost A layer of soil that is permanently frozen.

prospector A person who searches an area for mineral deposits, such as gold or silver.

refinery Industrial plant that purifies a substance, such as petroleum.

remote Far away; isolated.

settler A person who comes to live in an area.

strait A narrow body of water that connects two larger bodies of water.

taiga Forests in areas just outside the Arctic Circle or in areas with similar climates.

territory A geographic area belonging to a government.

tsar An emperor or ruler; the title of the leaders of Russia before 1917.

tundra Flat, treeless plains that have permanently frozen soil below the surface.

For More Information

Alaska Historical Society

P.O. Box 100299

Anchorage, AK 99510-0299

(907) 276-1596

Web site: http://www.alaskahistoricalsociety.org

This organization has many resources about Alaska's history.

Alaska Museum of Natural History

210 N. Bragaw Street

Anchorage, AK 99508

(907) 274-2400

Web site: http://www.alaskamuseum.org

Learn about Alaska's natural resources and animal and plant life by visiting this museum or its Web site.

Alaska Native Knowledge Network

University of Alaska Fairbanks

P.O. Box 756730

Fairbanks, AK 99775-6730

(907) 474-1902

Web site: http://www.ankn.uaf.edu

This organization has a wealth of information about Alaska's native people, their history, and their culture.

Anchorage Convention and Visitors Bureau

546 West Fourth Avenue

Anchorage, AK 99501-2212

(907) 276-4118

Web site: http://www.anchorage.net

Discover how much there is to do in Anchorage by contacting this bureau.

Klondike Gold Rush National Historical Park

P.O. Box 517

Skagway, AK 99840

(907) 983-2921

Web site: http://www.nps.gov/klgo/index.htm
The National Park Service runs a visitor's center in this park dedicated to the gold rush of 1898.

Office of the Governor

P.O. Box 110001
Juneau, AK 99811-0001
(907) 465-3500
Web site: http://www.gov.state.ak.us
Find out what is going on in Alaska's government. One can also contact the state's governor and his or her staff.

Web Sites

Due to the changing nature of Internet links, Rosen Publishing has developed an online list of Web sites related to the subject of this book. This site is updated regularly. Please use this link to access the list:

http://www.rosenlinks.com/uspp/akpp

FOR FURTHER READING

Armstrong, Jennifer. "1925: Mush!" *The American Story: 100 True Tales from American History*. New York, NY: A. A. Knopf, 2006.

Brown, Tricia. *Children of the Midnight Sun: Young Native Voices of Alaska*. Anchorage, AK: Alaska Northwest Books, 1998.

Bryan, Nichol. *Exxon Valdez Oil Spill* (Environmental Disasters). Milwaukee, WI: World Almanac Library, 2004.

Corwin, Jeff. *Into Wild Alaska* (The Jeff Corwin Experience). San Diego, CA: Blackbirch Press, 2004.

Crane, Carol. *L is for Last Frontier: An Alaska Alphabet*. Chelsea, MI: Sleeping Bear Press, 2002.

Gill, Shelley. *Iditarod Fact Book: A Complete Guide to the Last Great Race* (Alaska Book Adventures). Kenmore, WA: Epicenter Press, 2006.

Kupperberg, Paul. *The Alaska Highway* (Building America: Then and Now). New York, NY: Chelsea House, 2009.

Levinson, Nancy Smiler. *If You Lived in the Alaska Territory*. New York, NY: Scholastic, 1998.

London, Jack. *The Call of the Wild* (Oxford Children's Classics). New York, NY: Oxford University Press, 2009.

Miller, Debbie S. *Big Alaska: Journey Across America's Most Amazing State*. New York, NY: Walker & Co., 2006.

Orr, Tamra. *Alaska* (America the Beautiful). New York, NY: Children's Press, 2008.

Quasha, Jennifer. *How to Draw Alaska's Sights and Symbols* (A Kid's Guide to Drawing America). New York, NY: Powerkids Press, 2002.

Riddles, Libby. *Storm Run: The Story of the First Woman to Win the Iditarod Sled Dog Race*. Seattle, WA: Paws IV, 2002.

Stefoff, Rebecca. *Alaska* (Celebrate the States). New York, NY: Marshall Cavendish Benchmark, 2006.

Vanasse, Deb. *Out of the Wilderness*. New York, NY: Clarion Books, 1999.

Weber, Jen Funk. *Clueless in Alaska: Know More! An Activity Book Filled with Puzzles, Fun Facts, Games, and Jokes*. Seattle, WA: Sasquatch Books, 2006.

Winner, Cherie. *Life in the Tundra* (Ecosystems in Action). Minneapolis, MN: Lerner Publications Co., 2003.

BIBLIOGRAPHY

American Academy of Achievement. "Susan Butcher Biography." September 2, 2008. Retrieved September 6, 2009 (http://www.achievement.org/autodoc/page/but0bio-1).

Aversano, Earl J. "Leonhard Seppala: One Complex Man, One Stalwart Hero." 2009. Retrieved September 6, 2009 (http://www.baltostruestory.com/leonhardseppala.htm).

Biographical Directory of the U.S. Congress, 1774–Present. "Bartlett, Edward Lewis (Bob), (1904–1968)." Retrieved September 6, 2009 (http://bioguide.congress.gov/scripts/biodisplay.pl?index=b000201).

Borneman, Walter R. *Alaska: Saga of a Bold Land*. New York, NY: HarperCollins, 2003.

Braarud Fine Art. "Sydney Laurence." Retrieved September 6, 2009 (http://www.sydneylaurence.com/biography.html).

ExploreNorth. "Carl Ben Eielson, Alaska Aviation Pioneer." Retrieved September 6, 2009 (http://explorenorth.com/library/weekly/aa022800a.htm).

Gislason, Eric. "Senator E. L. 'Bob' Bartlett: Architect of Alaska Statehood." Retrieved September 6, 2009 (http://xroads.virginia.edu/~cap/BARTLETT/btintro.html).

Graef, Kris. *Alaska A to Z: A Handy Reference to the Places, People, History, Geography, and Wildlife of Alaska*. Bellevue, WA: Vernon Publications, 1997.

Haycox, Stephen W. *Alaska: An American Colony*. Seattle, WA: University of Washington Press, 2006.

IMDb.com. "Irene Bedard." 1990–2009. Retrieved September 6, 2009 (http://www.imdb.com/name/nm0065942).

Latino Legends in Sports. "Scott Gomez's Biography." 1999–2002. Retrieved September 6, 2009 (http://www.latinosportslegends.com/Gomez_Scott_bio.htm).

LitSite Alaska. "Austin Eugene 'Cap' Lathrop, 1865–1950." University of Alaska Anchorage, 2000–2009. Retrieved September 6, 2009 (http://www.litsite.org/index.cfm?section=Digital-Archives&page=Industry&cat=Media-and-Communications&viewpost=2&ContentId=2723).

NBA.com. "Carlos Boozer Bio." 2009. Retrieved September 6, 2009 (http://www.nba.com/playerfile/carlos_boozer/bio.html).

NBA.com. "Trajan Langdon Bio." 2009. Retrieved September 6, 2009 (http://www.nba.com/playerfile/trajan_langdon/bio.html).

Netstate.com. "Vitus Jonassen Bering." February 25, 2005. Retrieved September 6, 2009 (http://www.netstate.com/states/peop/people/ak_vjb.htm).

Official Home Page of Libby Riddles. "About Libby Riddles." Retrieved September 6, 2009 (http://www.libbyriddles.com/about.htm).

O'Malley, Julia. "Believe It or Not, Alaska's One of Nation's Least Religious States." *Anchorage Daily News*, July 13, 2008. Retrieved September 13, 2009 (http://www.adn.com/life/religion/story/463303.html).

OnRoute.com. "Skagway, Alaska: Gateway to the Klondike Gold Rush." Retrieved September 9, 2009 (http://www.onroute.com/destinations/alaska/skagway.html).

Ragan, John David. *The Explorers of Alaska* (World Explorers). New York, NY: Chelsea House, 1992.

Ritter, Harry. *Alaska's History: The People, Land, and Events of the North Country*. Anchorage, AK: Alaska Northwest Books, 1993.

Saleeby, Becky M. *The Quest for Gold: An Overview of the National Park Service Cultural Resources Mining Inventory and Monitoring Program (CRMIM)*. Anchorage, AK: U.S. Department of the Interior, National Park Service, 2000.

SportHaven.com. "Scott Gomez Career Biography and Statistics." Retrieved September 6, 2009 (http://www.sporthaven.com/players/scott-gomez).

Time. "Religion: Icebox Bishop." December 1, 1941. Retrieved September 6, 2009 (http://www.time.com/time/magazine/article/0,9171,802216,00.html).

Vanasse, Deb. "Deb Vanasse Biography." Retrieved September 6, 2009 (http://www.debvanasse.com/biography.html).

INDEX

A

Alaska
  animal life in, 5, 9, 11–12, 28
  economy of, 21, 26–29
  as the forty-ninth state, 20, 22
  geography of, 5, 6–11
  government of, 19, 22–25, 29
  history of, 5, 13–21
  as the Land of the Midnight Sun, 8
  as the Last Frontier, 5
  native people of, 5, 13–14, 21, 24, 32
  people from: past and present, 30–37
  plant life in, 12, 28
  religion and culture of, 32
  Russian presence in, 14–15, 16, 32
Alaska Highway, 19
Alaska Native Claims Settlement Act, 24
Aleut people, 14, 15, 19
Athabascan people, 13

B

Bartlett, E. L., 30
Bedard, Irene, 30
Boozer, Carlos, 31
Butcher, Susan, 31

C

civil rights, 24
Cook, James, 16

E

Eielson, Carl Ben, 31
executive branch, 22–23
Exxon Valdez, 9

F

farming, 27
Far North region, 6, 7–8
fishing industry, 24, 27

G

Gomez, Scott, 31, 33

H

house of representatives, 23

I

Iditarod, the, 18, 31, 36
Inside Passage, 11, 29
Interior region, 6, 8
Inuit, 13

J

Jackson, Sheldon, 32, 33
judicial branch, 22, 25

K

Kilcher, Jewel, 33
Klondike Gold Rush, 5, 17, 19, 34, 35

L

Langdon, Trajan, 34
Lathrop, Austin, 34
Laurence, Sydney, 34
legislative branch, 22, 23
Lindh, Hilary, 34
London, Jack, 35

M

Millenium Agreement of 2001, 24
mining industry, 17, 24, 26, 34

O

oil industry, 5, 9, 21, 24, 26, 28

P

Palin, Sarah, 35–36
Permanent Fund, 28
Prince William Sound, 9, 21

About the Author

Joanne Mattern has traveled throughout the United States and loves the immense variety in the nation. She enjoys history, nature, travel, and discovering new places and interesting stories. She has written more than two hundred nonfiction books for children and also works in her local library. Mattern enjoys spending time with her husband, four children, and a menagerie of pets.

Photo Credits

Cover (top left) Evans/Three Lions/Getty Images; cover (top right) Altrendo/Getty Images; cover (bottom) Lee Foster/Lonely Planet Images/Getty Images; pp. 3, 6, 13, 22, 26, 30 Michael Melford/The Image Bank/Getty Images; p. 4 © GeoAtlas; p. 7 Dave Houseknecht/USGS; p. 8 Mike Powell/Getty Images; p. 10 Melissa Farlow/National Geographic/Getty Images; p. 11 © www.istockphoto.com/Robert Plotz; pp. 14, 35 Hulton Archive/Getty Images; pp. 16, 20 (top) Library of Congress Prints and Photographs Division; p. 16 (bottom) ourdocuments.gov/National Archives; p. 17 Buyenlarge/Getty Images; p. 23 © Wasted Time R (talk)/Wikipedia; pp. 25, 27, 31 © AP Images; p. 28 USGS/Wikipedia; p. 29 Rich Reid/National Geographic/Getty Images; p. 33 J. Meric/Getty Images; p. 36 Stan Honda/AFP/Getty Images; p. 39 (left) Courtesy of Robesus Inc.; p. 40 (right and left) Wikipedia.

Designer: Les Kanturek; Editor: Andrea Sclarow;
Photo Researcher: Amy Feinberg

The Teacher Who Would Not Retire

To
Nicole Epstein,
Happy reading,
Sheila Sustrin~Letty Sustrin
February 9, 2004

Story by Sheila & Letty Sustrin
Illustrations by Thomas H. Boné III

Blue Marlin Publications

The Teacher Who Would Not Retire

Published by Blue Marlin Publications

Text copyright © 2002 by Sheila & Letty Sustrin

Illustrations copyright © 2002 by Francine Poppo Rich

First printing 2002

Publisher's Cataloging-in-Publication Data

Sustrin, Sheila.
   The teacher who would not retire / written by Sheila
and Letty Sustrin ; illustrated by Thomas H. Boné III
1st ed.
   p. cm.
   SUMMARY: When the principal tells first grade teacher
Mrs. Belle that she must retire, she and her students
wonder how they will keep in touch.
   Audience: Ages 4-8
   ISBN: 0-9674602-3-9

   1. Teachers--Juvenile fiction. 2. Retirement--
Juvenile fiction. [1. Teacher--Fiction. 2. Retirement
--Fiction.] I. Sustrin, Letty II. Bone, Thomas H. III. Title.

PZ7.S965875Te 2002   [E]

Blue Marlin Publications, Ltd.
823 Aberdeen Road, West Bay Shore, NY 11706
www.bluemarlinpubs.com

Printed and bound by Friesens Book Division in Altona, Manitoba, Canada
Book design & layout by Jude Rich

For
Eugene and Estelle
Special Parents
And
Louis Lotito and Pat Hudson
Special Principals
- LS & SS

To my loving wife Shantel for all of her wonderful support,

and to our beautiful daughter Ciana for her constant "Hey Dad"

greetings, which always put a smile on my face.

- THB

The sun was shining brightly when Mrs. Belle awakened. She stretched and said, "What a wonderful morning!" Mrs. Belle was the first grade teacher at the Laurelville Town School, and the children loved her. She always smiled and spoke softly to them, and she always shared her snacks with them.

Mrs. Belle opened her closet door. Ballet slippers covered every shelf. There were 10 pairs, and they were all different colors. "Let me see," said Mrs. Belle. "Which pair shall I wear today?"

She decided to wear the yellow ballet slippers, and as she danced into the classroom, all the children sang:

WE SEE YOU HERE! WE SEE YOU THERE!
WE SEE YOUR SLIPPERS EVERYWHERE!

BUT, all this happiness came to an end. Mr. Rivera, the Principal, looked very sad when he came into Mrs. Belle's classroom after school. He said, "Mrs. Belle, you know how we all love you. I am sorry, but I have to tell you that you must retire."

"What? Retire! Why?" shouted Mrs. Belle. "Who will teach the children that learning the alphabet and numbers can be fun? Who will show them how to share and be good friends? I must be there to read them their favorite stories. I cannot stop coming to this school."

Mr. Rivera said, "The School Rules say you are too old to teach at this school. Now you can stay home and rest. Please pack your things because the new teacher comes tomorrow."

Poor Mrs. Belle. She didn't even have a chance to say goodbye to the children. As she packed, she thought, "Who will get them ready for second grade?"

All night long, Mrs. Belle sat in her favorite cozy chair, thinking about what she should do. She had to make sure the children were happy at school.

Suddenly, she smiled. Mrs. Belle had a wonderful idea. She knew exactly what she was going to do tomorrow. She fell asleep feeling happy again.

The next morning, the children were so sad that Mrs. Belle had retired. They all cried and would not listen to the new teacher.

Suddenly, outside the window, the children saw the window washer peeking in. They all giggled because the window washer was wearing pink ballet slippers. IT WAS MRS. BELLE! They sang:

WE SEE YOU HERE! WE SEE YOU THERE!
WE SEE YOUR SLIPPERS EVERYWHERE!

"Hooray! Mrs. Belle is back," called the children, as they pressed themselves against the window.

Mr. Rivera heard the noise and came into the classroom. He said, "Mrs. Belle, you must leave at once!"

"NO! NO! I WILL NOT GO!" said Mrs. Belle. Mr. Rivera asked the crossing guard to walk Mrs. Belle away from the school.

But Mrs. Belle would not give up.

The next day, while the class was having lunch in the Cafeteria, there was a new food server. She did not look like Mrs. Belle, but all the children were whispering because the food server was wearing green ballet slippers. The children began singing:

WE SEE YOU HERE! WE SEE YOU THERE!
WE SEE YOUR SLIPPERS EVERYWHERE!

Mr. Rivera came marching in when he heard the children shouting, "Hooray! Mrs. Belle is back." He said, "Mrs. Belle, this will not do. You must leave right now."

"NO! NO! I WILL NOT GO!" said Mrs. Belle. This time the cook wheeled Mrs. Belle on a serving cart to her car.

The next morning, the fire inspector came to the school for a fire drill. He had a helper with him. When the children heard the fire bell ring, they walked quickly and quietly out of the building. All at once, the children pointed at the helper. She was wearing red ballet slippers. The children sang:

WE SEE YOU HERE! WE SEE YOU THERE!
WE SEE YOUR SLIPPERS EVERYWHERE!

Mr. Rivera said to the firefighters, "Take her away at once!" Mrs. Belle twirled around on her toes, fell backward, and landed in the firefighters' big, round net. As they carried her away,

Mrs. Belle kept shouting, "NO! NO! NO! I WILL NOT GO!"

When Mr. Rivera returned to his office, there was a whole line of Post Office workers putting sacks of mail all over the room. "What is all this mail?" asked Mr. Rivera.

One mail carrier said, "These are letters from the parents. There's one from me too. We decided to write them because we don't want Mrs. Belle to retire."

"Oh, what am I going to do?" said Mr. Rivera. "I must call a meeting and see how we can solve this problem and make everyone happy."

That night, the parents and children were invited to a special meeting in the school gym.

Mr. Rivera stood on stage, smiled, and said, "Our School Board has a very special job for Mrs. Belle. From now on, every Friday will be "Mrs. Belle Day" at the Laurelville Town School. We have made a cozy corner in our library, and we will invite Mrs. Belle to read her favorite stories to the children."

The school cheerleaders lined up in front and shouted a cheer for Mrs. Belle:

MRS. BELLE, HOORAY! HOORAY!
YOU'RE COMING BACK FOR READING DAY!

DISTRICT MEETING

Mr. Rivera announced, "I wish Mrs. Belle were here to see how much she is loved. She would be so happy." The children pointed and sang:

WE SEE YOU HERE! WE SEE YOU THERE!
WE SEE YOUR SLIPPERS EVERYWHERE!

The cheerleader in the middle was wearing silver ballet slippers!

Mrs. Belle danced around the Gym, smiling and hugging everyone. "You have made me so happy tonight," said Mrs. Belle. "I can't wait for Friday to come."

Sometimes the books are about learning new things, and sometimes they're about having good manners.

But Mrs. Belle always makes it a fun time.

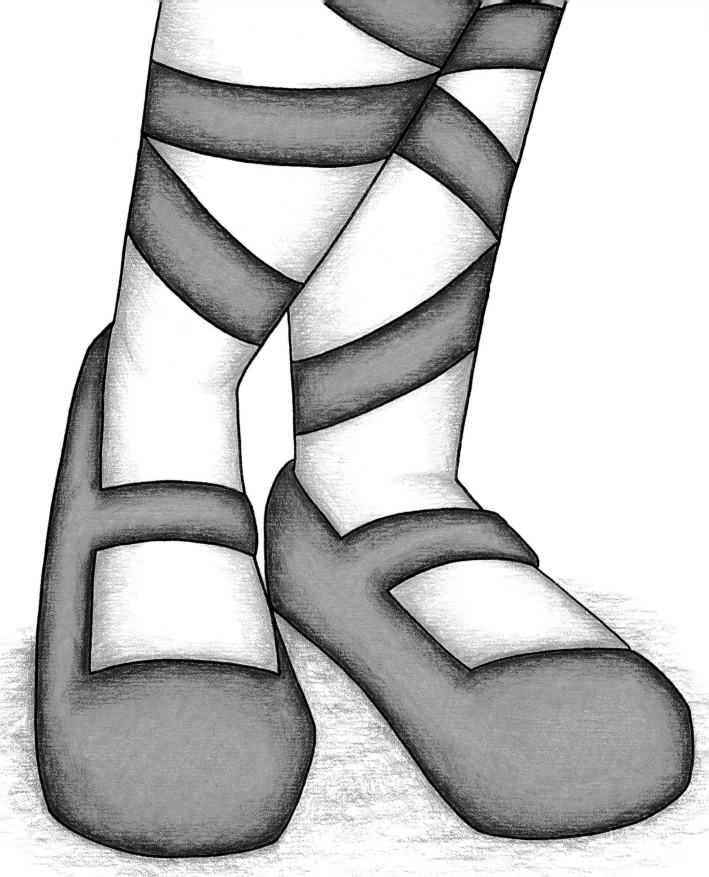

And, of course, she always wears her ballet slippers.

MRS. BELLES
CAT

THE
NURSE DISGUISE

THE CONSTRUCTION
WORKER DISGUISE

THE
TRAPEZE
ARTIST
DISGUISE

NO
DISGUISE!
THE ORIGINAL
MRS. BELLE

THE
JAZZ
PLAYER
DISGUISE